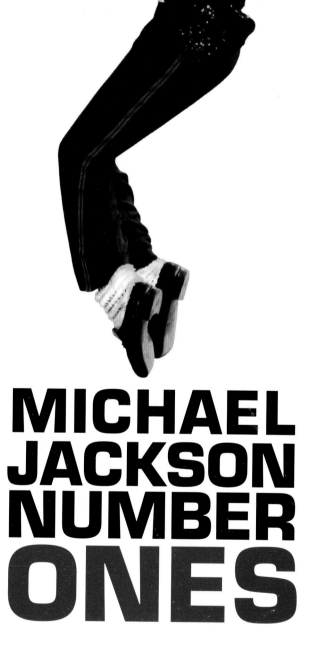

D0760442

MICHAEL JACKSON NUMBER ONES

Project Manager: CAROL CUELLAR

Album Art © 2003 MJJ Productions Inc.
© 2004 WARNER BROS. PUBLICATIONS
All Rights Reserved

Any duplication, adaptation or arrangement of the compositions
contained in this collection requires the written consent of the Publisher.
No part of this book may be photocopied or reproduced in any way without permission.
Unauthorized uses are an infringement of the U.S. Copyright Act and are punishable by law.

CALGARY PUBLIC LIBRARY

OCT   2005

SHAWNESSY BRANCH

CONTENTS

BAD

Written and Composed by
MICHAEL JACKSON

* These chords contain no 3rds.

Bad - 8 - 1

© 1987 MIJAC MUSIC (BMI)
All Rights Administered by WARNER-TAMERLANE PUBLISHING CORP. (BMI)
All Rights Reserved

*Sing the lyrics between the asterisks 2nd time only.

12

Additional Lyrics
(For repeat)

You know I'm smooth–I'm
bad–you know it
(Bad bad–really, really bad)
You know I'm bad–I'm
bad baby
(Bad bad–really, really bad)
You know, you know, you
know it–come on
(Bad bad–really, really bad)
And the whole world has to
answer right now
(And the whole world has to
answer right now)
Woo!
(Just to tell you once again)

You know I'm bad, I'm bad–
you know it
(Bad bad–really, really bad)
You know I'm bad–you know-hoo!
(Bad bad–really, really bad)
You know I'm bad–I'm bad–
you know it, you know
(Bad bad–really, really bad)
And the whole world has to
answer right now
(And the whole world has to
answer right now)
Just to tell you once again...
(Just to tell you once
again...)
Who's bad?

BEAT IT

Written and Composed by
MICHAEL JACKSON

They told him, "Don't you ev - er
They're out to get you. Bet - ter

come a - round here. Don't wan - na see your face; you bet - ter dis - ap-pear."
leave while you can. Don't wan - na be a boy; you wan - na be a man.
The
You

Beat It - 3 - 1

© 1982 MIJAC MUSIC (BMI)
All Rights Administered by WARNER-TAMERLANE PUBLISHING CORP. (BMI)
All Rights Reserved

BEN

Words by
DON BLACK

Music by
WALTER SCHARF

© 1971, 1972 (Renewed 1999, 2000) JOBETE MUSIC CO., INC.
All Rights Controlled and Administered by EMI APRIL MUSIC INC.
All Rights Reserved   Used by Permission

BILLIE JEAN

Written and Composed by
MICHAEL JACKSON

Billie Jean - 4 - 1

© 1982, 1983 MIJAC MUSIC
All Rights Administered by WARNER-TAMERLANE PUBLISHING CORP. (BMI)
All Rights Reserved

BLACK OR WHITE

Written and Composed by
MICHAEL JACKSON

© 1991 MIJAC MUSIC (BMI)
All Rights Administered by WARNER-TAMERLANE PUBLISHING CORP. (BMI)
All Rights Reserved
Rap Lyrics Written by BILL BOTTRELL © 1991 IGNORANT MUSIC
All Rights Administered by WB MUSIC CORP.
All Rights Reserved

I am tired of this dev - il, I am tired of this stuff.

I am tired of this bus - iness, sew when the go-ing gets rough.

I ain't scared of your broth - er, I ain't scared of no sheets.

BREAK OF DAWN

Written and Composed by
MICHAEL JACKSON and DR. FREEZE

© 2001 Mijac Music and Sony/ATV Songs LLC/Uncle James Music
All Rights for Mijac Music Administered by Warner-Tamerlane Publishing Corp.
All Rights Reserved

Verse 1:

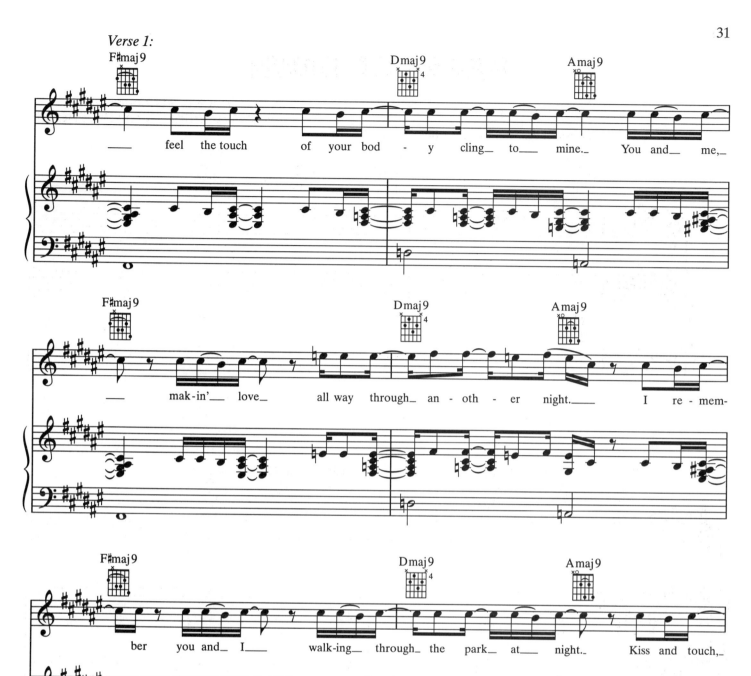

feel the touch of your bod - y cling to mine. You and me, mak-in' love all way through an - oth - er night. I re-mem-

ber you and I walk-ing through the park at night. Kiss and touch,

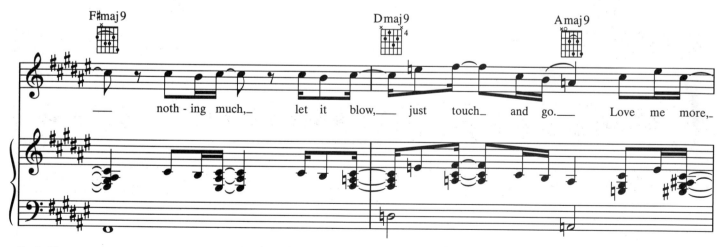

noth-ing much, let it blow, just touch and go. Love me more,

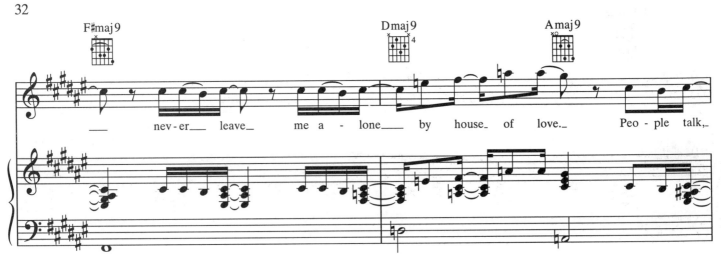

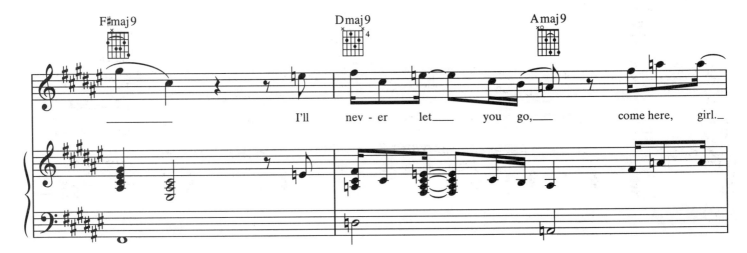

Chorus:

36

Bridge:

Let's not wait, the sun__ is out, let's get up__ and let's__ get out. It's the day,__

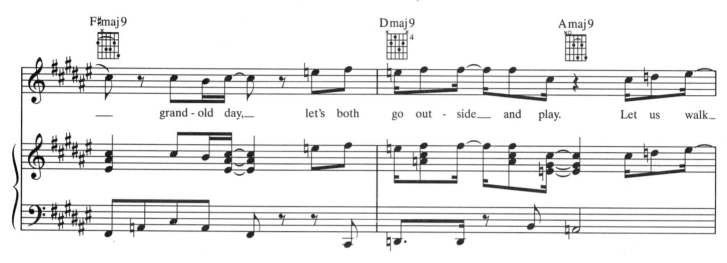

__ grand - old day,__ let's both go out - side__ and play. Let us walk__

__ down__ the park,__ mak-in' love__ 'til__ it's dark.__ Let me move__

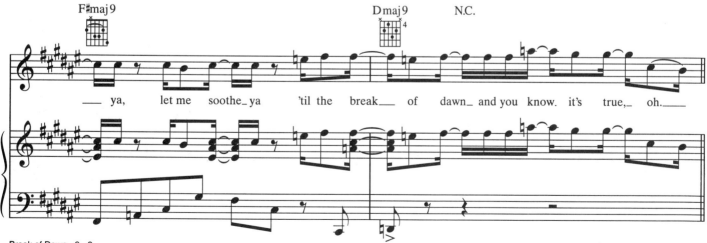

__ ya, let me soothe__ ya 'til the break__ of dawn__ and you know. it's true,__ oh.__

I JUST CAN'T STOP LOVING YOU

Written and Composed by
MICHAEL JACKSON

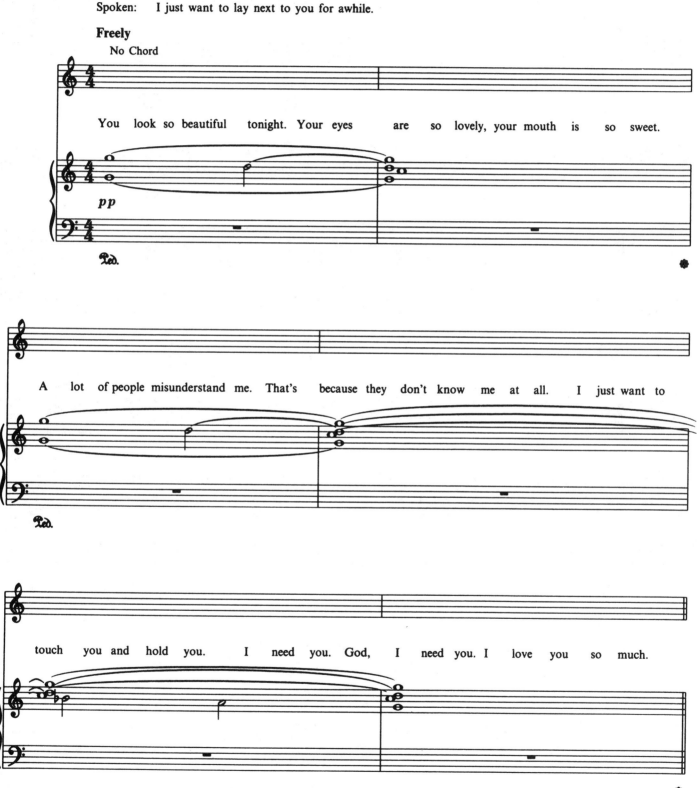

Spoken: I just want to lay next to you for awhile.

Freely

No Chord

You look so beautiful tonight. Your eyes are so lovely, your mouth is so sweet.

pp

A lot of people misunderstand me. That's because they don't know me at all. I just want to

touch you and hold you. I need you. God, I need you. I love you so much.

I Just Can't Stop Loving You - 7 - 1

© 1987 MIJAC MUSIC (BMI)
All Rights Administered by WARNER-TAMERLANE PUBLISHING CORP. (BMI)
All Rights Reserved

Sung: *(Michael)*

Each time the wind ___ blows, I hear your voice, ___ so

I call your name.

Whis-pers at morn - ing,

our love is dawn - ing, heav-en's glad ___ you came. ___

the love   you bring.
a love   so true.   (Siedah): When Heav-en's in my ___ heart,   at morn-ing a-wakes ___ me,   will

your call I hear ___ harps,   and   an - gels   sing. ___
you come and take ___ me?   I'll   wait for   you. ___

___   (Michael): You know how I feel,   this thing can't go wrong.
You know how I feel,   I   feel,   I won't stop un - til

I can't live my life with - out you. ___   (M): I
I hear your voice say - ing I do.   (Siedah): (I   do.)   This

44

Additional Lyrics (for Repeat and Fade)

(Both): I just can't stop loving you.
(Michael): Hee! Hee! Hee! Know I do, girl.
(Both): I just can't stop loving you.
(Michael): You know I do. And if I stop,
(Both): Then tell me just what will I do?

DIRTY DIANA

Written and Composed by
MICHAEL JACKSON

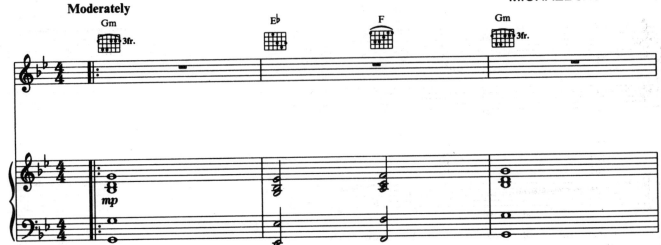

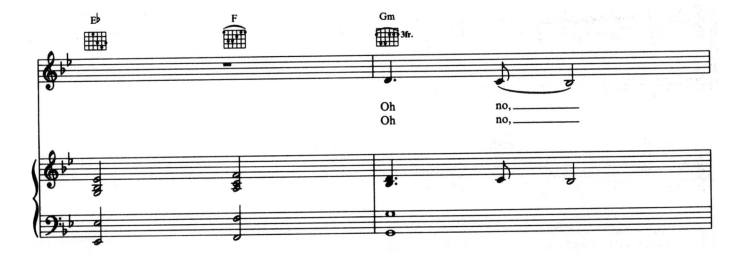

Oh   no,_____
Oh   no,_____

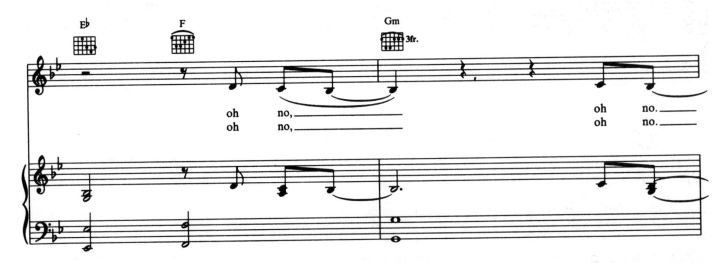

oh   no,_____   oh   no._____
oh   no,_____   oh   no._____

© 1987 MIJAC MUSIC
All Rights Administered by WARNER-TAMERLANE PUBLISHING CORP.
All Rights Reserved

You'll nev - er make me stay,___ so take your
She likes the boys in the band,___ she knows when
She said I have to go home,___ 'cause I'm when real

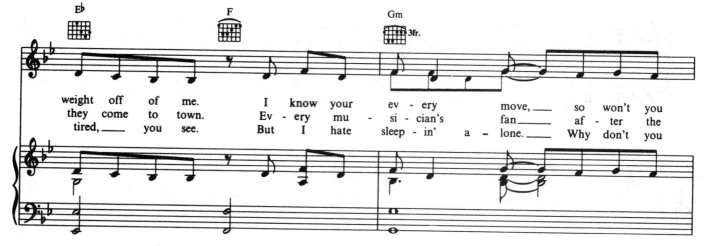

weight off of me. I know your ev - ery move,___ so won't you
they come to town. Ev - ery mu - si - cian's fan___ af - ter the
tired,___ you see. But I hate sleep - in' a - lone.___ Why don't you

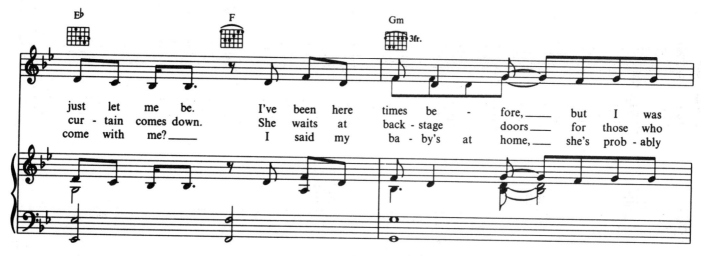

just let me be. I've been here times be - fore,___ but I was
cur - tain comes down. She waits at back - stage doors___ for those who
come with me?___ I said my ba - by's at home,___ she's prob - ably

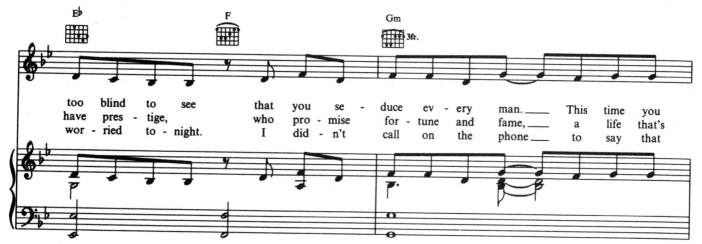

too blind to see that you se - duce ev - ery man.___ This time you
have pres - tige, who pro - mise for - tune and fame,___ a life that's
wor - ried to - night. I did - n't call on the phone___ to say that

* Sing the lyrics, "Dirty Diana, nah." twice, last time only.

DON'T STOP 'TIL YOU GET ENOUGH

Written and Composed by
MICHAEL JACKSON

Moderately slow ♩ = 102

N.C.

mf (Spoken:) You know I was, I was wondering, you know, that if we should keep on, because the force, it,

it's got a lot of power, and you make me feel like, you make me feel like... oo.

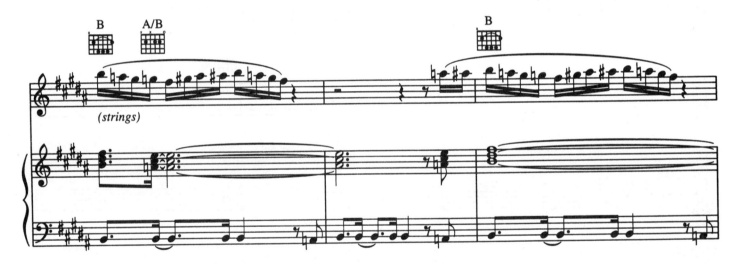

B   A/B

(strings)

B

A/B

Don't Stop 'Til You Get Enough - 8 - 1

© 1979 MIRAN MUSIC (BMI)
All Rights Administered by WARNER-TAMERLANE PUBLISHING CORP. (BMI)
All Rights Reserved

Pow - er _____ is the force, the__ vow _____
melt - ing _____ like hot can - dle - wax. _____
3. Heart - break, _____ en - e - my des - pise. _____

___ that makes it hap - pen, _____ and there's no
___ Sen - sa - tion _____ love - ly
___ E - ter - nal _____ love shines

ques - tions__ why.____ Oo,____ get clo - ser _____
where we're_ at.____ Oo,____ so let love _____
in my__ eyes.____ Oo,____ so let love _____

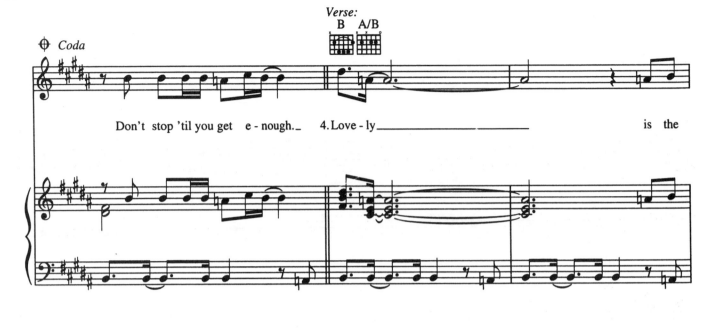

Don't stop 'til you get e - nough.__ 4. Love - ly_____ is the

feel - ing__ now._____ I won't_ be com-plain - ing,_

the force is love pow - er._____ Oo.__ Keep on__

EARTH SONG

Written and Composed by
MICHAEL JACKSON

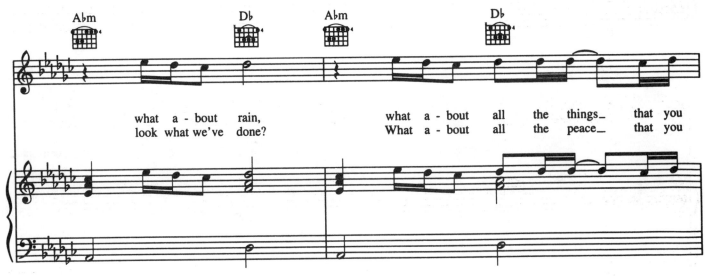

1. What a - bout sun - rise,
2. What have we done to the world,

what a - bout rain,
look what we've done?

what a - bout all the things that you
What a - bout all the peace that you

Earth Song - 6 - 1

© 1995 MIJAC MUSIC (BMI)
All Rights Administered by WARNER-TAMERLANE PUBLISHING CORP. (BMI)
All Rights Reserved

said we were_ to gain?__
pledge your on - ly son?__
What a - bout kill - ing fields,
What a - bout flow-ering fields,
is there a time,
is there a time?

what a - bout all the things_ that you said was yours_ and mine?__ Did you
What a - bout all the dreams_ that you said was yours_ and mine?__ Did you

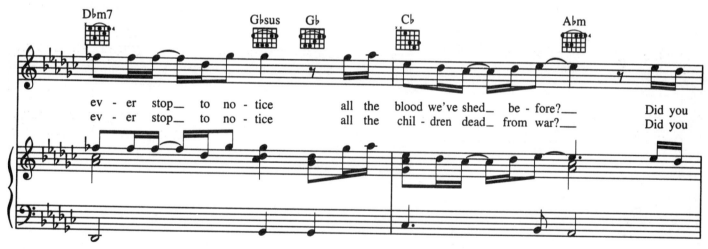

ev - er stop_ to no - tice all the blood we've shed_ be - fore?__ Did you
ev - er stop_ to no - tice all the chil - dren dead_ from war?__ Did you

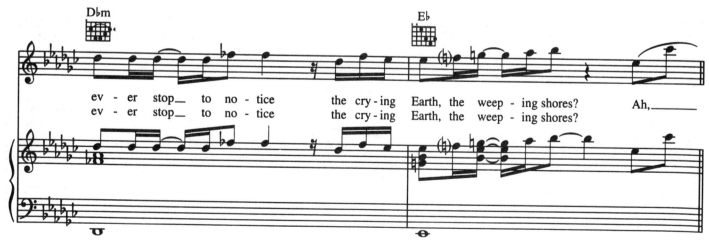

ev - er stop_ to no - tice the cry - ing Earth, the weep - ing shores?
ev - er stop_ to no - tice the cry - ing Earth, the weep - ing shores?
Ah,_____

62

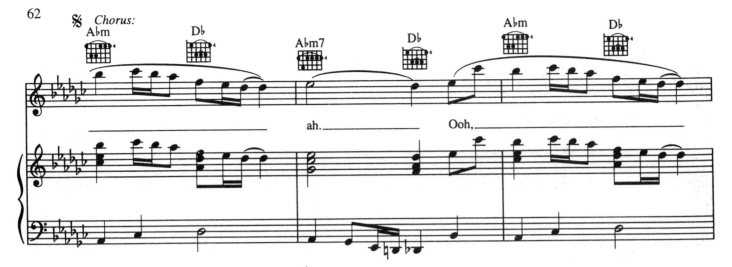

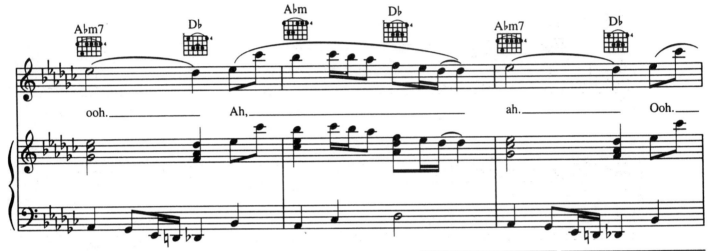

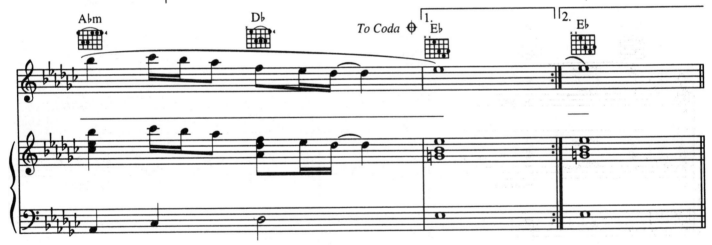

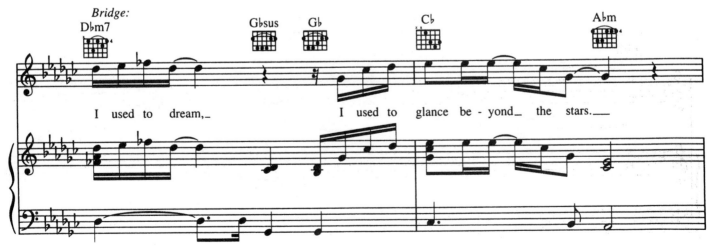

D.S. % al Coda

Now I don't know_ where we are,_ al - though I know we've drift - ed far._
Ah,___

⊕ Coda

_ Ah,_____ ah.____ Ooh,___

_____ ooh.____ Ah,_____

ah._____ Ooh._____ 1. Hey,_____

Verse 2:
What about animals?
  (What about it?)
We've turned kingdoms to dust?
  (What about us?)*
What about elephants?
Have we lost their trust?
What about crying whales?
We're ravaging the seas.
What about forest trails,
  (Ooh, ooh.)
Burnt despite our pleas?

Verse 3:
What about the holy land
  (What about it?)
Torn apart by creed?
What about the common man,
Can't we set him free?
What about children dying?
Can't you hear them cry?
Where did we go wrong?
  (Ooh, ooh.)
Someone tell me why.

Verse 4:
What about babies
  (What about it?)
What about the days?
What about all their joy?
What about the man?
What about the crying man?
What about Abraham?
What about death again?
  (Ooh, ooh.)
Do we give a damn?
(To Chorus:)

*Repeat after every line except where specified.

MAN IN THE MIRROR

Words and Music by
SIEDAH GARRETT and GLEN BALLARD

Man in the Mirror - 13 - 1

© 1987 Yellowbrick Road Music, Universal - MCA Music Publishing,
A Division of Universal Studios, Inc. and Aerostation Corporation
All Rights for Yellowbrick Road Music Administered by WB Music Corp.
All Rights for Aerostation Corporation Administered by Universal - MCA Music Publishing,
A Division of Universal Studios, Inc.
All Rights Reserved

As I turn up the col-lar on__ my fav-orite win-ter coat,__ this wind is blow-in' my mind.__ I see the kids__ in the street__ with not e-nough to eat. Who am I to be blind? Pre-tend-ing not to see their__ needs.__

Am7(addD)

A sum-mer's dis-re-gard,

G/B

a bro-ken bot-tle top,

Man in the Mirror - 13 - 2

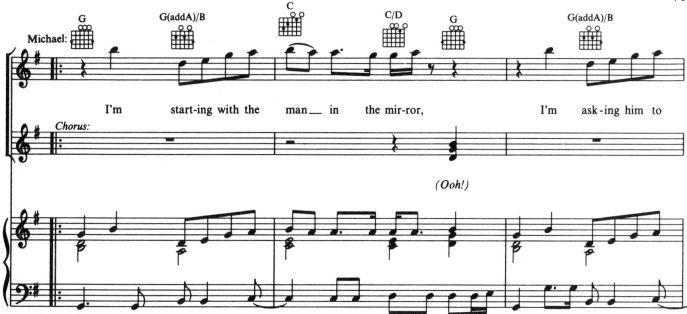

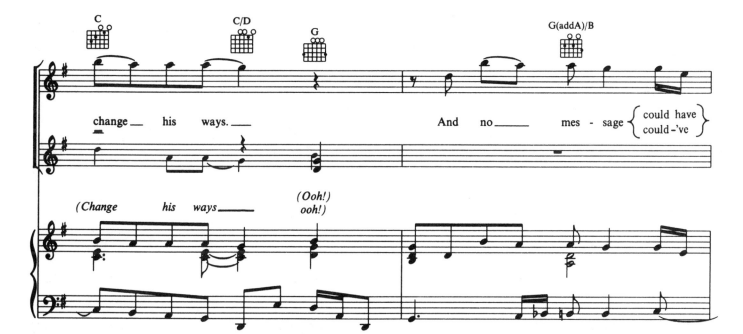

Man in the Mirror - 13 - 12

Additional Lyrics for repeat:
(Yeah!-Make that change)
You know-I've got to get
 that man, that man...
(Man in the mirror)
You've got to
You've got to move! Come
 on! Come on!
You got to...
Stand up! Stand up!
 Stand up!
(Yeah!-Make that change)
Stand up and lift
 yourself, now!
(Man in the mirror)
Hoo! Hoo! Hoo!
Aaow!
(Yeah!-Make that change)
Gonna make that change...
 come on!
You know it!
You know it!
You know it!
You know...
(Change...)
Make that change.

ONE MORE CHANCE

Words and Music by
R. KELLY

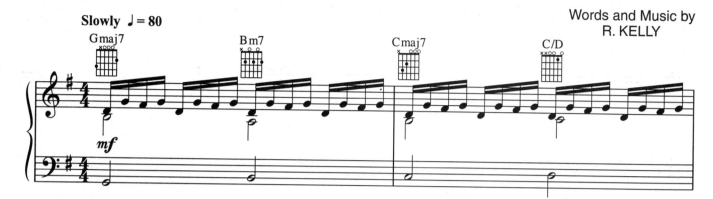

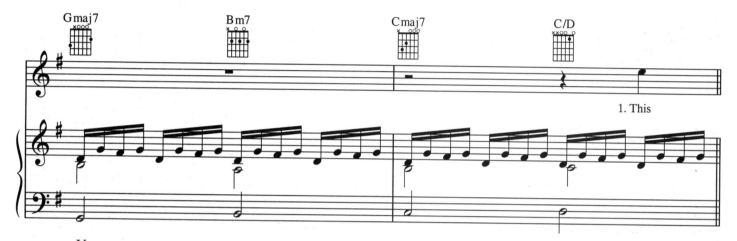

1. This

Verse:

time,
ing

I'm gon-na do my best to make it right.
for that one who's gon-na make me whole,

Can't go on with-out you by my side.
help me make these mys-ter-y's un-fold.

Hold on.
Hold on.

Shel-
Light-

One More Chance - 5 - 1

© 2003 Zomba Songs Inc. (BMI)/ R. Kelly Publishing, Inc. (BMI)
All Rights for the world on behalf of R. Kelly Publishing, Inc. (BMI) Administered by Zomba Songs Inc. (BMI)
All Rights Reserved

One— more chance— at— love. One— more chance— at— love.

One— more chance— at— love. One— more chance— at— love.

1.

One— more chance— at— love. One— more chance— at— love.

2. Search -

Bridge:

2.

One— more chance— at— love. And I will walk a-round this world,— to

find__ her,__ and I don't care what it takes,__ no.____ (Why?_)

I'd sail the sev - en seas to be near her. And if you

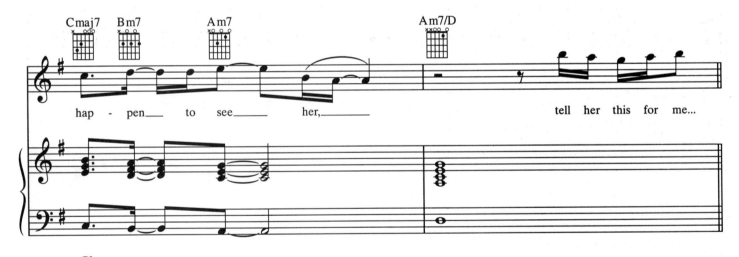

hap - pen__ to see____ her,_____ tell her this for me...

Chorus:

One__ more chance_ at__ love. One__ more chance_ at__ love.

One__ more chance__ at__ love. One__ more chance_ at__ love.

One__ more chance_ at__ love. One__ more chance_ at__ love.

Repeat ad lib. and fade

One__ more chance_ at__ love. One__ more chance_ at__ love.

ROCK WITH YOU

Words and Music by
ROD TEMPERTON

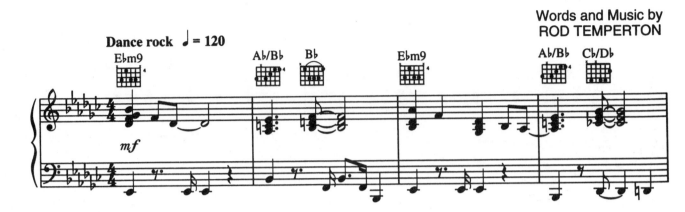

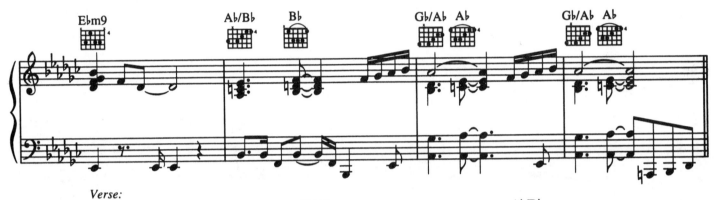

Verse:

1. Girl, close your eyes, let that rhy-thm get in-to you.
2. Out on the floor,_ there ain't no-bod-y there but us.

you.
us.

Don't try to fight___ it, there ain't

Girl,___ when you dance, there's a

Rock With You - 5 - 1

© 1979 RODSONGS
All Rights Administered by ALMO MUSIC CORP.
All Rights Reserved   Used by Permission

noth - in' that you can do.
mag - ic that must be— love.—
Re - lax— your mind,—
Just take— it slow,—

—— lay back— and groove— with mine.— You got - ta
'cause we got— so far— to go.— When you

feel that heat and we can } ride the boo-gie. Share that beat of love.— I wan-na
feel that heat and we're gon-na }

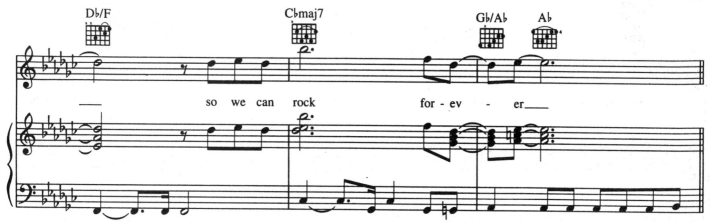

THE WAY YOU MAKE ME FEEL

Medium Rock

Written and Composed by
MICHAEL JACKSON

© 1987 MIJAC MUSIC (BMI)
All Rights Administered by WARNER-TAMERLANE PUBLISHING CORP. (BMI)
All Rights Reserved

90

* **Second time only.**

The Way You Make Me Feel - 9 - 4

Go on girl!   Go on!

Hee! ____ Hee!   Aaow!

Go on girl!

D.S. 𝄋 *(Lyric 2) al Coda* ✠

The Way You Make Me Feel - 9 - 5

94

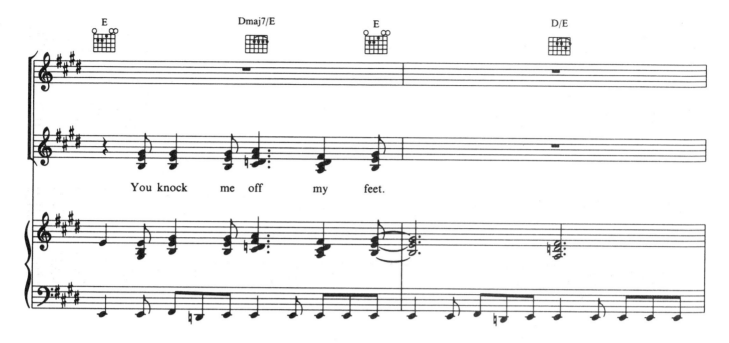

You knock me off my feet.

My lone - ly days are gone.

Additional Lyrics for repeat:
Ain't nobody's business.
  ain't nobody's business
(The way you make me feel)
Ain't nobody's business.
Ain't nobody's business but
  mine and my baby
(You really turn me on)
Hee hee!
(You knock me off of
  my feet)
Hee hee! Ooh!
(My lonely days are gone)
Give it to me-give me
  some time
(The way you make me feel)
Come on be my girl-I wanna
  be with mine
(You really turn me on)
Ain't nobody's business-

(You knock me off of
  my feet)
Ain't nobody's business but
  mine and my baby's
Go on girl! Aaow!
(My lonely days are gone)
Hee hee! Aaow!
Chika-chika
Chika-chika-chika
Go on girl-Hee hee!
(The way you make me feel)
Hee hee hee!
(You really turn me on)
(You knock me off my feet)
(My lonely days are gone)
(The way you make me feel)
(You really turn me on)
(You knock me off my feet)
(My lonely days are gone)

SMOOTH CRIMINAL

Written and Composed by
MICHAEL JACKSON

Moderately

Smooth Criminal - 12 - 1

© 1987 MIJAC MUSIC
All Rights Administered by WARNER-TAMERLANE PUBLISHING CORP.
All Rights Reserved

So they came in-to the out-way, it was Sun-day — What a black day.

Mouth to mouth re-sus-ci-ta-tion, sound-ing heart-beats — in-tim-i-da-tions.

An-nie, are you O K? So An-nie, are you O K? Are you O K, An-nie?

108

Smooth Criminal - 12 - 11

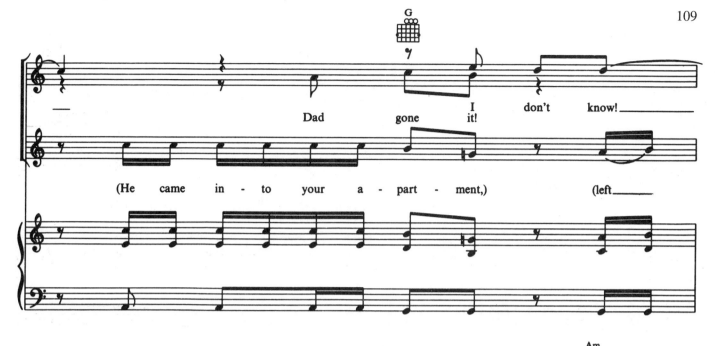

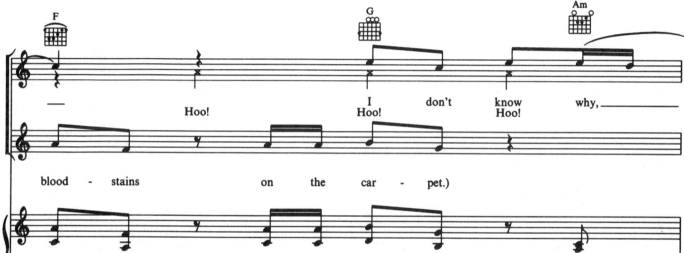

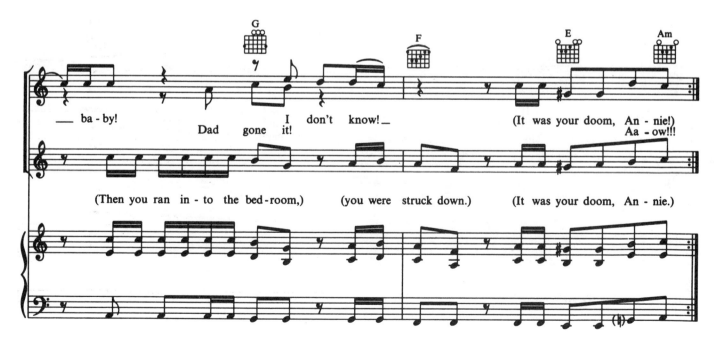

Smooth Criminal - 12 - 12

THRILLER

Words and Music by
ROD TEMPERTON

It's close to mid - night,___ and some-thin' e - vil's lurk - in' in the dark.___
You hear the door___ slam___ and re - al - ize there's no-where left to run.___
They're out to get___ you.___ There's de - mons clos - in' in on ev - 'ry side.___

Thriller - 6 - 1

© 1982 RODSONGS
All Rights Administered by ALMO MUSIC CORP.
All Rights Reserved   Used by Permission

Un - der the moon - light _____ you
You feel the cold _____ hand, _____ and
They will pos - sess _____ you _____ un -

see a sight that al-most stops your heart. _____ You try to scream, _____ but
won-der if you'll ev-er see the sun. _____ You close your eyes, _____ and
less you change that num-ber on your dial. _____ Now is the time _____ for

ter - ror takes_ the sound_ be-fore_ you make_ it. _____ You start to freeze_
hope that this_ is just_ i - mag - i - na - tion._ But all the while,_
you and I _____ to cud - dle close_ to-geth - er._ All thru the night_

as   hor-ror looks_you right_ be-tween_ the eyes.__   You're par-a-lyzed.__
you   hear the crea-ture creep-in' up__ be-hind.__   You're out of time.__
I'll   save you from_ the ter-ror on__ the screen.__   I'll make you see __

'Cause this is   thrill - er,__   thrill - er   night,   and
'Cause this is   thrill - er,__   thrill - er   night.   There
that this is   thrill - er,__   thrill - er   night,   'cause

no   one's gon-na   save__   you from the beast__   a-bout to strike.__ You know, it's
ain't no sec-ond chance__ a-gainst the thing__ with for-ty eyes.__ You know, it's
I   could thrill you more__ than an-y ghost__ would dare to try.__ Girl, this is

RAP: Darkness falls across the land.
The midnight hour is close at hand.
Creatures crawl in search of blood
To terrorize y'awl's neighborhood.
And whosoever shall be found
Without the soul for getting down
Must stand and face the hounds of hell
And rot inside a corpse's shell.

The foulest stench is in the air,
The funk of forty thousand years,
And grizzly ghouls from every tomb
Are closing in to seal your doom.
And though you fight to stay alive,
Your body starts to shiver,
For no mere mortal can resist
The evil of a thriller.

YOU ARE NOT ALONE

Written and Composed by
R. KELLY

© 1995 ZOMBA SONGS INC./R. KELLY PUBLISHING, INC. (Adm. by ZOMBA SONGS INC.)
All Rights Reserved

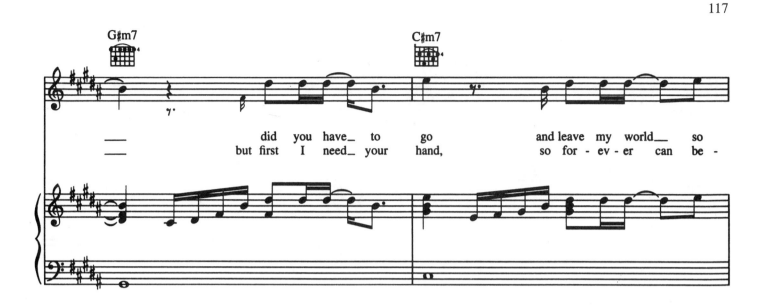

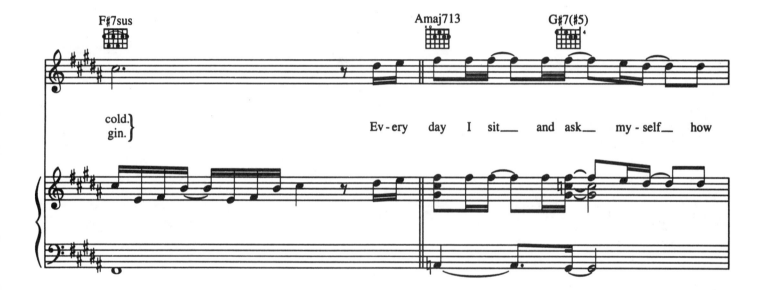

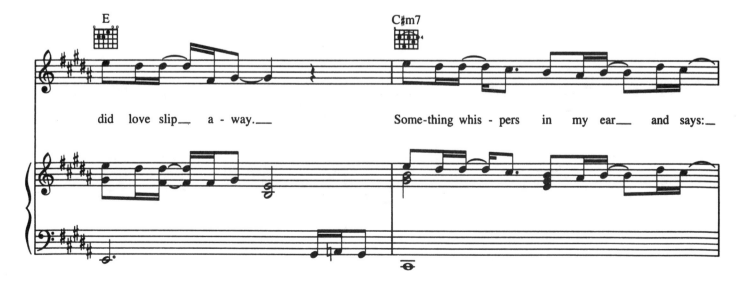

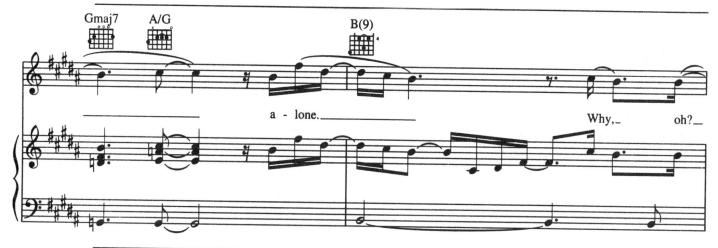

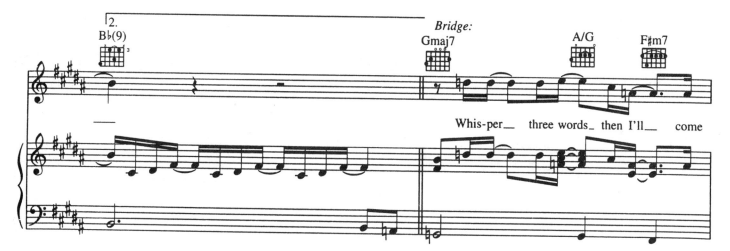

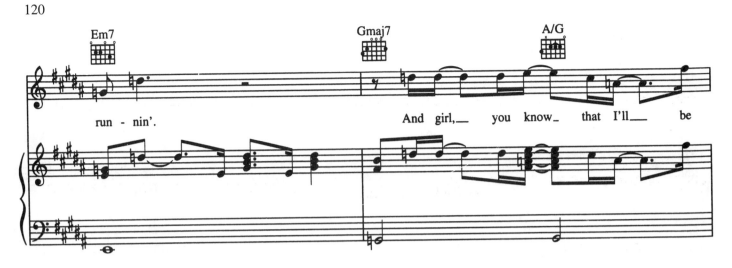

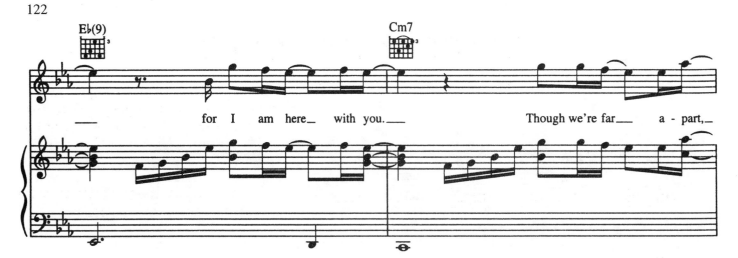

for I am here___ with you.___   Though we're far___ a - part,___

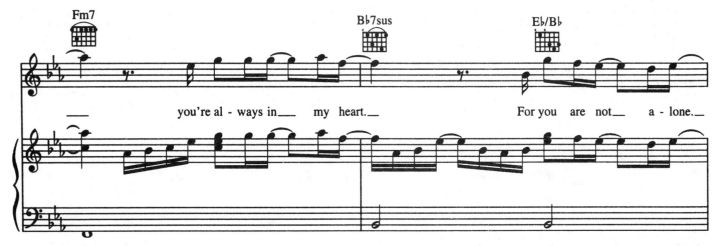

you're al - ways in___ my heart.   For you are not___ a - lone.___

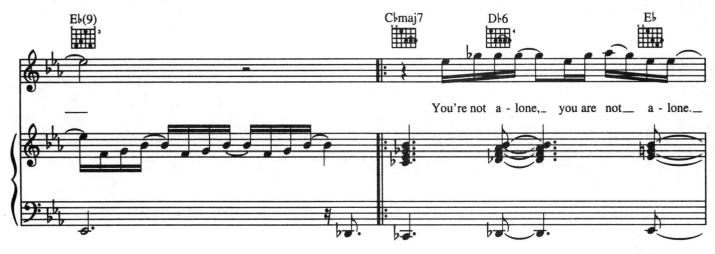

You're not a - lone,___ you are not___ a - lone.___

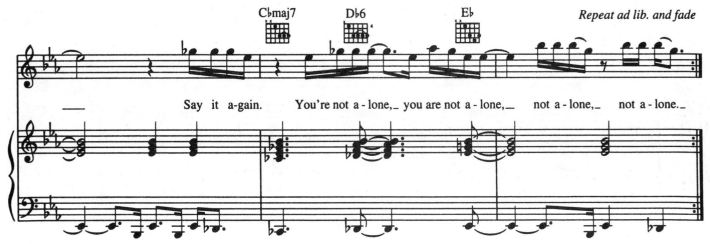

Repeat ad lib. and fade

Say it a-gain.   You're not a - lone,___ you are not a - lone,___ not a - lone,___ not a - lone.___

You Rock My World

Written and Composed by
MICHAEL JACKSON, RODNEY JERKINS,
FRED JERKINS III, LASHAWN DANIELS
and NORA PAYNE

© 2001 Mijac Music, EMI Blackwood Music Inc./Rodney Jerkins Productions Inc.,
Ensign Music Corporation/Fred Jerkins Publishing, EMI April Music Inc./LaShawn Daniels Productions Inc., and Generations Third Music Publishing
All Rights for Mijac Music Administered by Warner-Tamerlane Publishing Corp.
All Rights Reserved

Verse 2:
In time, I knew that love would bring
Such happiness to me.
I tried to keep my sanity.
I've waited patiently.
Girl, you know it seems
My life is so complete.
A love that's true because of you.
Keep doing what you do.
Think that I found the perfect love
I've searched for all my life.
(Searched for all my life.)
Think I'd find such a perfect love
That's awesomely so right, girl.
(To Chorus:)